Ukulele *from the* Beginning
Pop Songs
The Blue Book

T0039693

CHESTER MUSIC

Published by
Chester Music
14-15 Berners Street,
London W1T 3LJ, UK.

Order No. CH81136
ISBN 978-1-78305-120-5
This book © Copyright 2013 Chester Music.
All rights reserved. International copyright secured.

Book content and layout by Camden Music.
Compiled by Christopher Hussey.
Edited by Toby Knowles.

About the series

This songbook uses the chords and picking patterns taught in *Ukulele from the Beginning Book 2*. As well as making this an ideal companion book for anyone working through the *Ukulele from the Beginning* course, *Pop Songs: The Blue Book* is also an enjoyable standalone song collection for anyone learning to play the ukulele. Even an absolute beginner will find this collection of new and classic pop songs very accessible and easy to follow.

Contents

About this book

Here's a great selection of pop songs to add to your repertoire! They use only what you have learnt in *Ukulele From The Beginning Books 1* and *2*, featuring all of the chords that you know by the end of *Book 2*, as well as the strumming and fingerpicking patterns you have been taught.

Below are the fingerpicking patterns that you'll need for songs in this book, and opposite is a library of all the chords used.

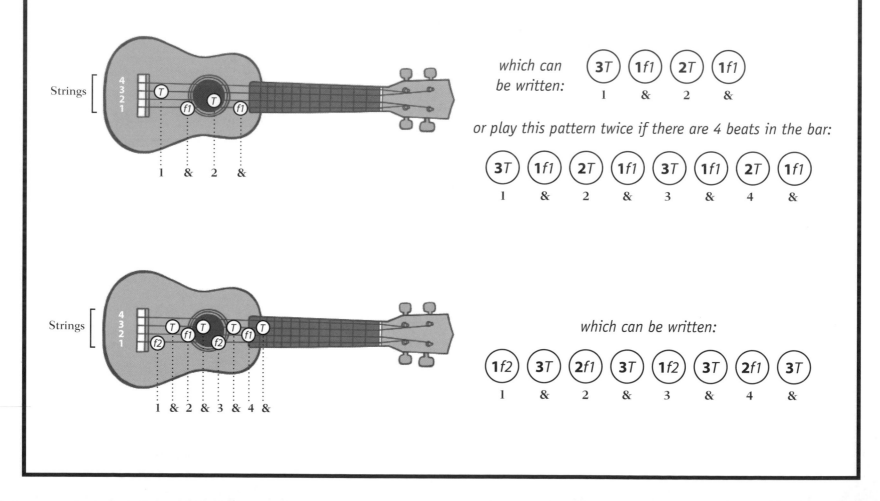

Chord Library

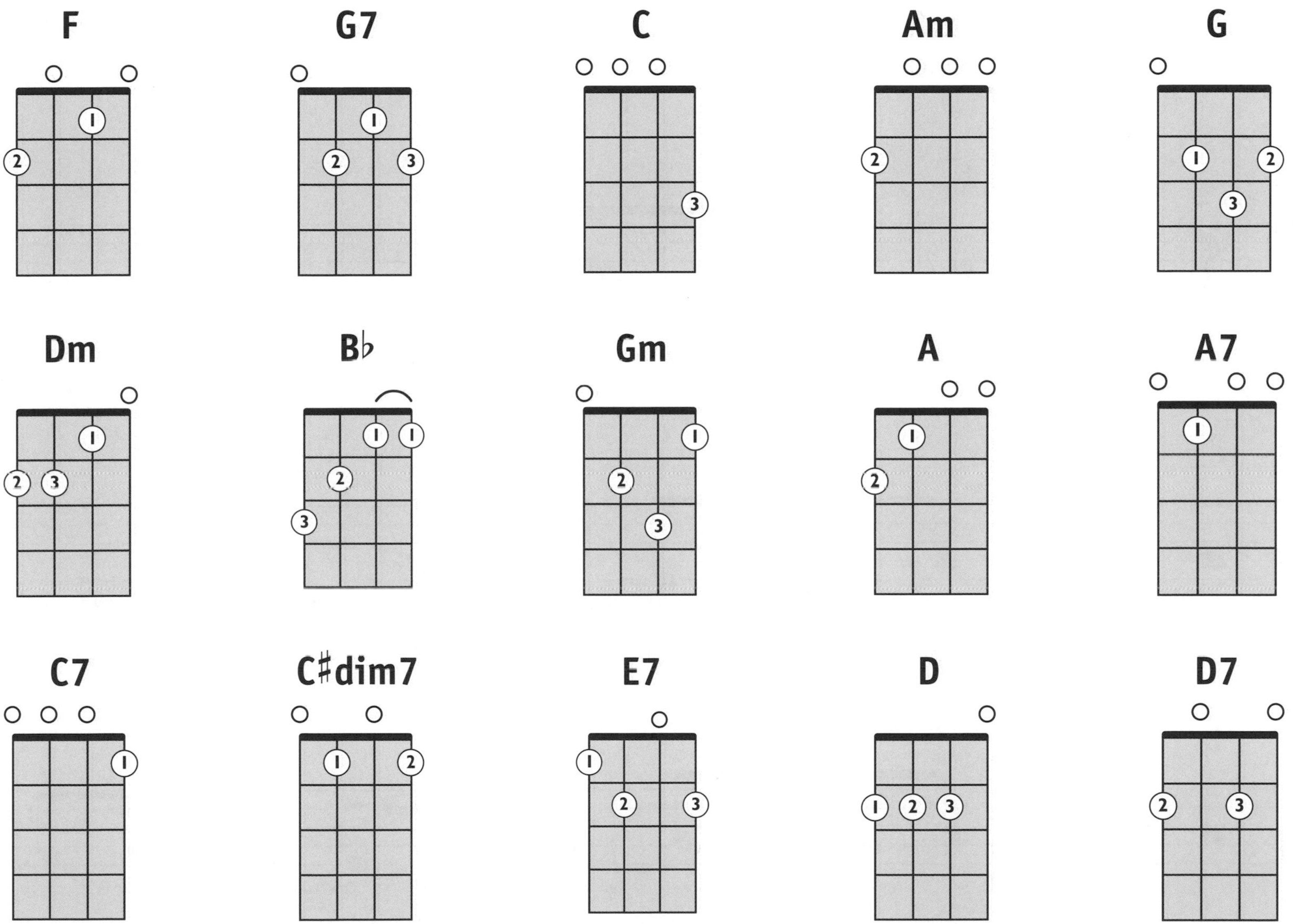

F

G7

C

Am

G

Dm

B♭

Gm

A

A7

C7

C♯dim7

E7

D

D7

Viva La Vida

Words & Music by Guy Berryman, Jon Buckland, Will Champion & Chris Martin

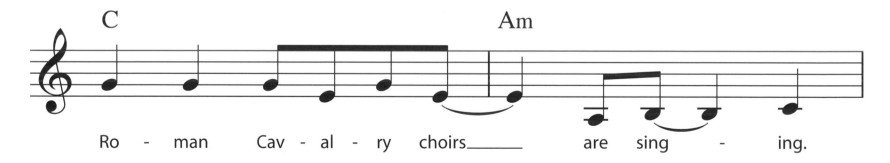

I hear Jer - u - sal - em bells_____ a - ring - ing.

Ro - man Cav - al - ry choirs_____ are sing - ing.

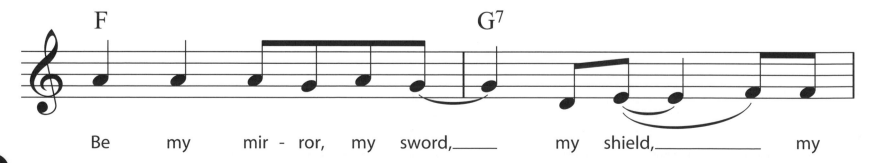

Be my mir - ror, my sword,_____ my shield,_____ my

The Sound Of Silence

Words & Music by Paul Simon

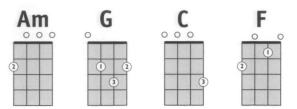

Hel - lo   dark - ness,   my   old   friend,_____

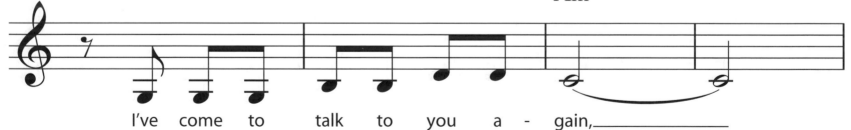

I've   come   to   talk   to   you   a - gain,_____

be - cause   a   vis - ion,   soft - ly   creep - ing,_____

left   its   seeds while   I   was   sleep   -   ing.____

And   the   vis - ion_____   that   was   plant - ed____

in   my____   brain_____   still   re - mains_____

with - in   the   sound_____   of   si - lence.____

Love Story

Words & Music by Taylor Swift

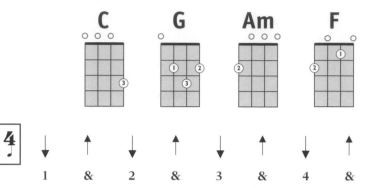

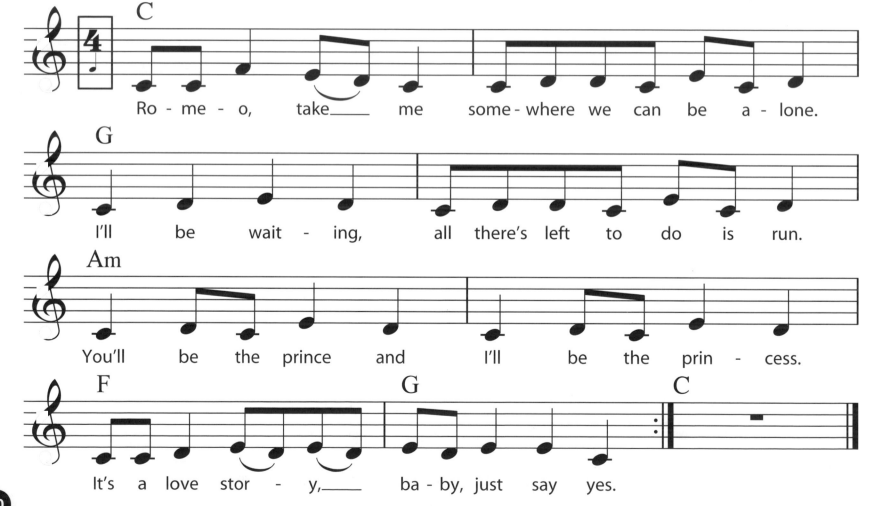

Ro - me - o, take____ me some - where we can be a - lone.

I'll be wait - ing, all there's left to do is run.

You'll be the prince and I'll be the prin - cess.

It's a love stor - y,____ ba - by, just say yes.

Mad World

Words & Music by Roland Orzabal

One More Night

Words & Music by Savan Kotecha, Adam Levine, Martin Max & Johan Schuster

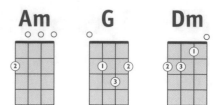

Am

Ba - by, there you go a - gain, there you go a - gain,
you stuck on my bod - y, on my bod - y,

G   **Dm**

ma - king me love you._____ Yeah,
like a tat - too._____ And

Am

I stopped u - sing my head, u - sing my head,
now I'm feel - in' stu - pid, feel - in' stu - pid,

Bleeding Love

Words & Music by Ryan Tedder & Jesse McCartney

Call My Name

Words & Music by Calvin Harris

How d'you think I feel when you call my name? You got me con - fused____ by the way I change. How d'you think I feel when you call my____ name,____ my name? Say my name, ba - by.

Run

Words & Music by Gary Lightbody, Jonathan Quinn, Mark McClelland,
Nathan Connolly & Iain Archer

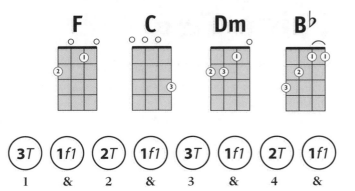

Light up,＿ light up,＿ as if you＿ have＿
Loud - er,＿ loud - er,＿ and we'll run＿ for＿

＿ a choice; e - ven if you can - not＿ hear＿ my voice,
＿ our lives. I can hard - ly speak, I＿ un - der - stand why

I'll be right be - side you＿ dear.＿
you can't raise your voice to＿ say...

Price Tag

Words & Music by Lukasz Gottwald, Claude Kelly, Bobby Ray Simmons & Jessica Cornish

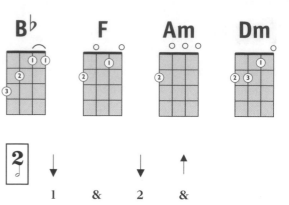

It's not a - bout the mon - ey, mon - ey, mon - ey,___

___ we don't need your mon - ey, mon - ey, mon - ey;___

___ we just wan - na make the world dance,___

for - get a - bout the price tag._____ Ain't a - bout the...

cha - ching,_____ cha - ching, ain't a - bout the

b - bling,_____ b - bling; wan - na make the world dance,__

for - get a - bout the price tag._____

Fireflies

Words & Music by Adam Young

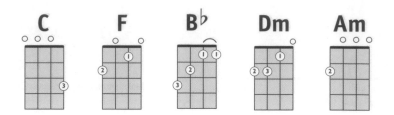

You would__ not be - lieve your eyes   if ten__ mil-lion

fire   –   flies   lit   up   the world__ as I fell a - sleep.__

__   'Cause they'd__ fill   the   o - pen air   and leave tear-drops

ev - 'ry - where; you'd think_____ me rude, but I_____ would just stand and

stare._____ I'd like to make my - self be - lieve_____

that plan - et Earth turns slow - ly. It's

hard to say___ that I'd rath - er___ stay a - wake when I'm___ a - sleep, be -

- cause my dreams are burst - ing at___ the seams._____

Can You Feel The Love Tonight

(from Walt Disney Pictures' 'The Lion King')

Words by Tim Rice & Music by Elton John

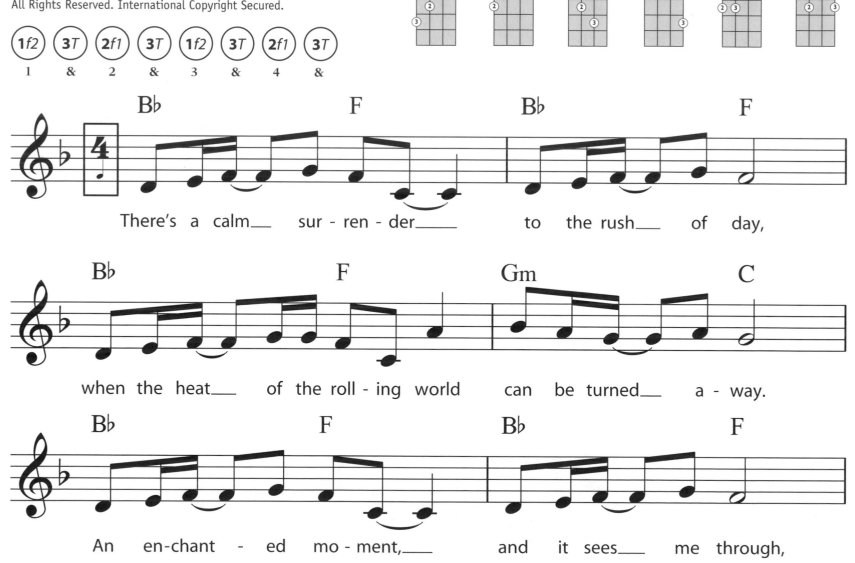

There's a calm___ sur - ren - der___ to the rush___ of day,

when the heat___ of the roll - ing world can be turned___ a - way.

An en-chant - ed mo - ment,___ and it sees___ me through,

Troublemaker

Words & Music by Stephen Robson, Claude Kelly, Olly Murs & Flo Rida

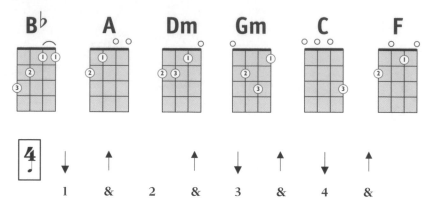

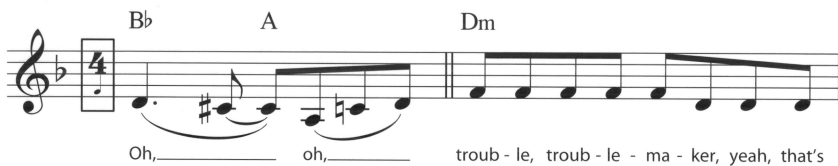

Oh,_____ oh,_____ troub - le, troub - le - ma - ker, yeah, that's

your mid - dle name.__ Oh,_____ I know you're no good but you're

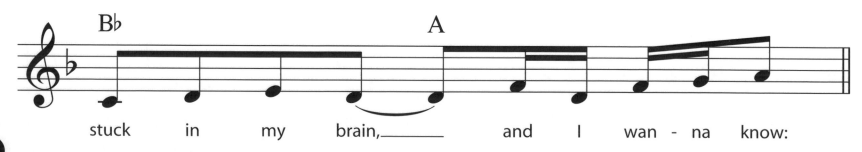

stuck in my brain,_____ and I wan - na know:

Locked Out Of Heaven

Words & Music by Ari Levine, Philip Lawrence & Peter Hernandez

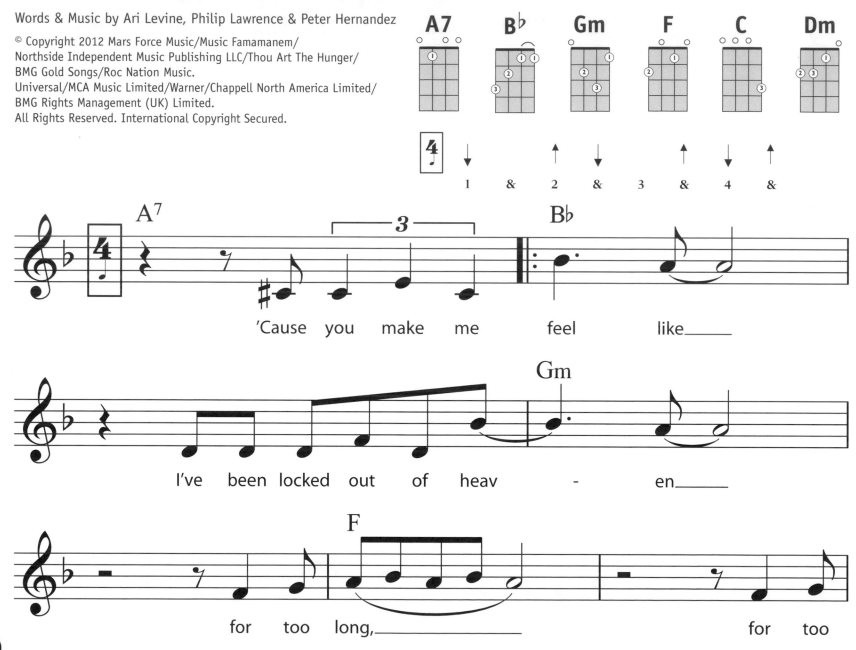

'Cause you make me feel like____

I've been locked out of heav - en____

for too long,____ for too

Isn't She Lovely

Words & Music by Stevie Wonder

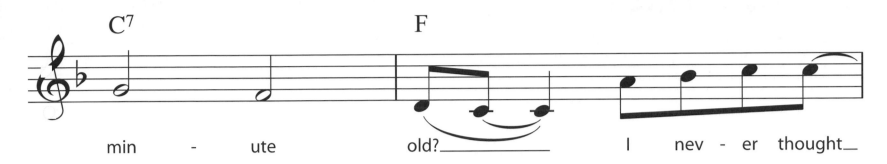

min - ute   old?_____   I   nev - er thought__

____ through love   we'd be_____   ma - king

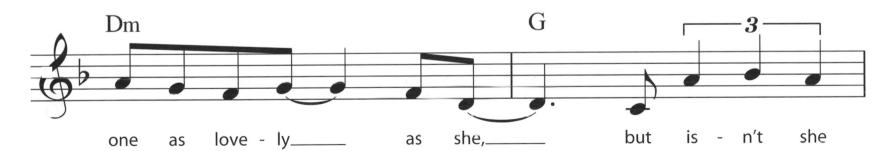

one   as   love - ly_____   as   she,_____   but   is - n't she

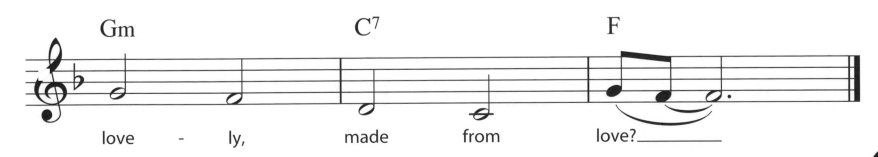

love - ly,   made   from   love?_____

Video Games

Words & Music by Elizabeth Grant & Justin Parker

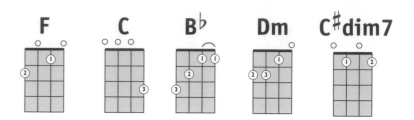

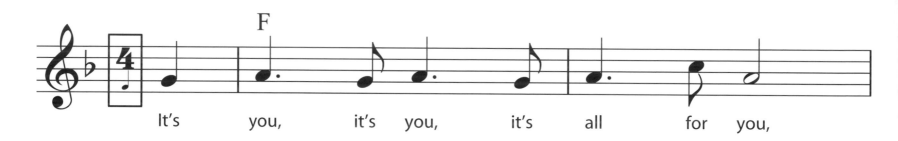

It's   you,   it's   you,   it's   all   for   you,

ev – 'ry-thing   I   do.   I   tell   you   all   the   time,   heav-en   is   a

place   on   Earth   with   you.___   Tell   me   all   the   things   you   wan - na   do.__

Yesterday

Words & Music by John Lennon & Paul McCartney

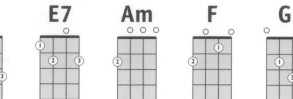

Yes - ter - day,___ all my troub - les seemed so far a - way.___

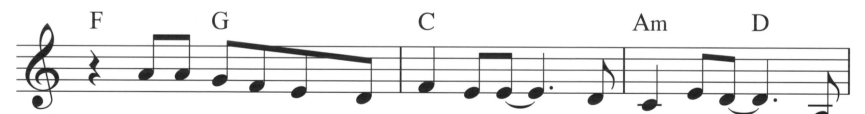

Now, it looks as though they're here to stay.___ Oh, I be - lieve___ in

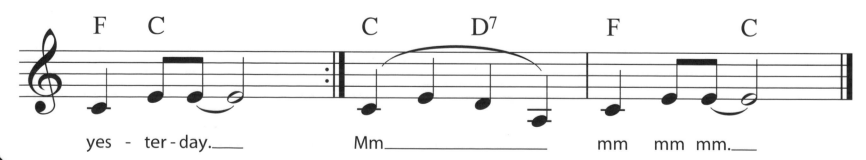

yes - ter - day.___ Mm___ mm mm mm.___

123456789